# HOW TO DRAW
# ROBOTS AND ALIENS

## Janet Cook

Edited by Judy Tatchell

Designed by Mary Forster and Nigel Reece

Illustrated by Kuo Kang Chen and Keith Hodgson

Additional illustrations by Peter Scanlan and Chris Reed

## Contents

# About this book

This book is packed with ideas for drawing robots and aliens. You can also find out how to create textures, from a thick, leathery skin to polished metal.

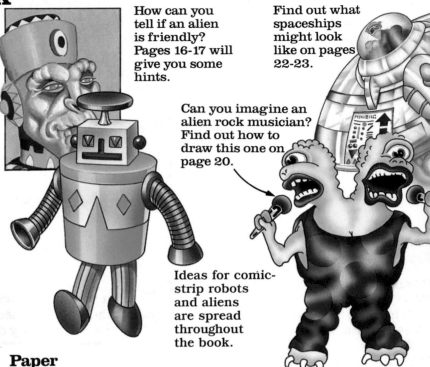

How can you tell if an alien is friendly? Pages 16-17 will give you some hints.

Find out what spaceships might look like on pages 22-23.

Can you imagine an alien rock musician? Find out how to draw this one on page 20.

Ideas for comic-strip robots and aliens are spread throughout the book.

## Pencils

Drawing is easier if you have the right pencil for the job. Hard pencils are good for neat edges and detail. Softer ones are good for shading.

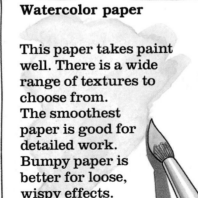

This thin lead is good for details and outlines.

This is good for general drawing.

This is good for shading small areas neatly.

Use this soft lead to shade large areas.

You can tell how hard a pencil is by looking at the marking on its side. H stands for hard, and B stands for black, which means the pencil has a soft lead.

2H

H

2B

6B

## Paper

For sketches, any scrap paper will do, but for a really professional look, it is a good idea to invest in some art paper. Here are some types to look for. A good art shop will also give you advice.

### Watercolor paper

This paper takes paint well. There is a wide range of textures to choose from. The smoothest paper is good for detailed work. Bumpy paper is better for loose, wispy effects.

### Bristol paper

This is even less textured than the smoothest watercolor paper. It is a good choice when you are using wax or pencil crayons, but paint tends to run on it.

## One step at a time...

Most of the drawings in the book are broken down into two or three stages for you to follow. For example, the diagrams below show how to draw a spaceship.

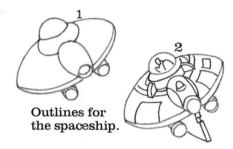

Outlines for the spaceship.

Always draw the lines shown in green first, then the red ones. Remember to erase any lines that are not on the finished image.

## Coloring materials

There are lots of different materials you can choose from to color your pictures. Here are some of them.

Drawing inks can be applied with a brush or an ink pen. They are good for details.

Gouache paints give you a stronger, flatter look than watercolors.

## How to stop paper from wrinkling

When you paint, paper gets wet and stretches slightly. Then as it dries, it shrinks. This can cause watercolor paper to wrinkle. To prevent this from happening, you can stretch the paper before you paint on it.

1.  Position the paper on some board. Use a brush or sponge to wet it all over with clean water.

2.  Smooth the paper flat, then tape it to the board. Let it dry, then remove it from the board.

Tape down all four sides.

You can buy pre-stretched paper, or thick paper that does not need stretching. However, it is usually quite expensive.

Pastels are like soft sticks of chalk. They blend together smoothly, but are too thick for detailed work.

Watercolor paints are useful for creating texture, or for a subtle, delicate look.

Pencil crayons come in many colors. You use the tip for details, and the side for shading.

Poster paints are similar to gouache. Although cheaper, there are not as many colors.

Thick wax crayons are good for large areas. They leave a shiny finish.

# First robots

You can get ideas for drawing robots by looking at everyday objects and making them come alive. The robots below have tin cans for their bodies.

They have been painted with a specialized artists' tool known as an airbrush. You can achieve a similar effect with paints.

Tin can shape

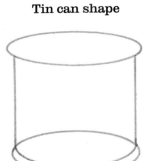

A curved window makes the robot look rounded.

The lines shown by dashes are not on the finished picture.

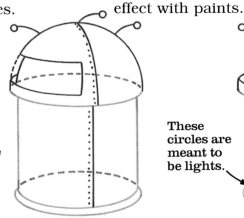

These circles are meant to be lights.

**1.** Using your pencil, copy this tin can shape. To make the sides really straight, use a ruler or the side of a book.

**2.** Draw a dome for the head. Add an eye window, antennae, a seam line and some tiny bolts. Erase the lines shown by dashes.

**3.** Now draw some rectangles and circles on the robot's body. Add two more lines and a row of bolts on its head.

Pincer

Go over the whole outline in thin black felt tip.

Pale patches look like shiny metal.

Leave part of each light white.

You can find out more about how to make things shiny on pages 8-9.

Dark color for shadow.

Add a gray area beneath the wheel to make the robot stand on the ground.

**4.** Draw two tubes for each arm, then add circular shapes for the shoulders, elbows and wrists. Now add some pincers.

**5.** Finally, add a base and two wheels under the robot.

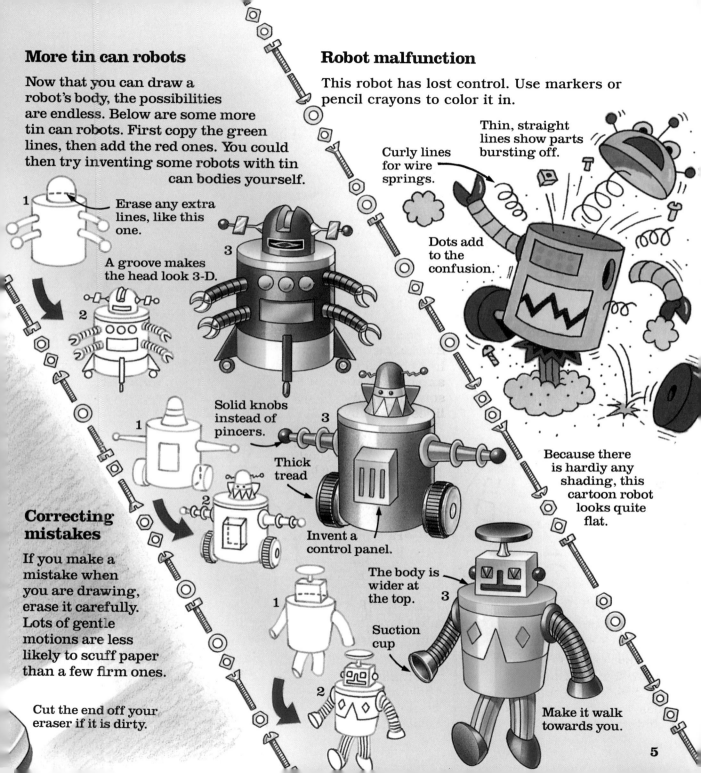

## More tin can robots

Now that you can draw a robot's body, the possibilities are endless. Below are some more tin can robots. First copy the green lines, then add the red ones. You could then try inventing some robots with tin can bodies yourself.

1

Erase any extra lines, like this one.

A groove makes the head look 3-D.

2

3

Solid knobs instead of pincers.

1

Thick tread

2

3

Invent a control panel.

## Correcting mistakes

If you make a mistake when you are drawing, erase it carefully. Lots of gentle motions are less likely to scuff paper than a few firm ones.

Cut the end off your eraser if it is dirty.

## Robot malfunction

This robot has lost control. Use markers or pencil crayons to color it in.

Thin, straight lines show parts bursting off.

Curly lines for wire springs.

Dots add to the confusion.

Because there is hardly any shading, this cartoon robot looks quite flat.

1

2

3

The body is wider at the top.

Suction cup

Make it walk towards you.

5

# More difficult robots

You can make impressive robots out of geometric shapes. Here is an octagonal (eight-sided) robot, and a more rounded one. They have been painted to look realistic, with shadows and highlights to give them shape.

The animal robots opposite are colored in a simpler, flatter style. This style is more suitable for cartoons.

The tips below will help you to achieve a good finish with poster paints or watercolors.

## Painting tips

- Use several thin layers of paint, rather than one thick layer.

- For a crisp finish, let the paint dry between layers.

- For a soft look, add each new layer while the previous one is still slightly damp.

- Once the final layer is dry, you can add highlights and touch up shadows with pencil crayons.

Studs give the appearance of solid metal.

The shading makes the ear look hollow.

Add thin blue tubes to join the arm sections.

Color the edges of the arms darker. This makes them look shiny.

The head is bigger than the lower body.

You can only see part of this shoulder.

1. Draw the chest and some shoulders. Add half rings for the neck and waist, and boxes for the head and lower body.

2. Draw three tubes for each arm, and circles for the hands. Add the ear boxes and wheels, and copy the red lines around the chest.

3. Draw the face and ear cups. Turn the hands into pincers, then add the finishing touches to the rest of the body.

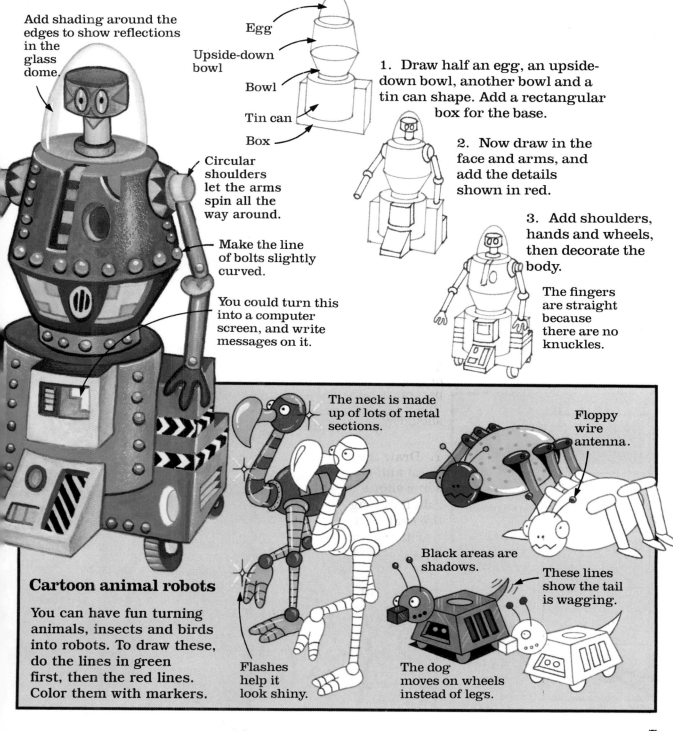

Add shading around the edges to show reflections in the glass dome.

Egg

Upside-down bowl

Bowl

Tin can

Box

1. Draw half an egg, an upside-down bowl, another bowl and a tin can shape. Add a rectangular box for the base.

Circular shoulders let the arms spin all the way around.

2. Now draw in the face and arms, and add the details shown in red.

Make the line of bolts slightly curved.

You could turn this into a computer screen, and write messages on it.

3. Add shoulders, hands and wheels, then decorate the body.

The fingers are straight because there are no knuckles.

The neck is made up of lots of metal sections.

Floppy wire antenna.

**Cartoon animal robots**

You can have fun turning animals, insects and birds into robots. To draw these, do the lines in green first, then the red lines. Color them with markers.

Flashes help it look shiny.

Black areas are shadows.

These lines show the tail is wagging.

The dog moves on wheels instead of legs.

# Androids

Many of the robots you see in science fiction movies look like human beings. These are called androids. Below you can find out how to draw and paint a really hi-tech android. There are also some cartoon androids for fun.

## Drawing your android

1. Start with this outline. Press gently so you can erase it later.

2. Now make the robot more solid. Erase any hidden green lines.

3. Add the blue lines to give it joints and pull it together.

## Preparing a palette

First choose the color you want to use for the android. Mix white paint with it in the amounts shown below so that you end up with four shades plus pure white.

1. Pure green

2. ¾ green ¼ white

3. ½ green ½ white

4. ¼ green ¾ white

5. Pure white

## Painting your android

Before starting, you have to decide which direction you want the light to come from. You will then know which areas are shady and which are bright. Here, it is coming from the right.

1. Take your darkest shade and paint the areas on the robot which would not catch any light.

2. Paint a strip alongside the area you have just painted, using the second darkest shade.

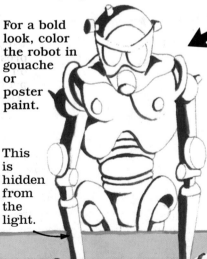

For a bold look, color the robot in gouache or poster paint.

This is hidden from the light.

Light comes from this direction.

Use lines (hatching) or dots (stippling) to blend the colors.

# Cartoon androids

You can have great fun turning people into robots. Here are a couple to start you off. Remember to draw the outlines in pencil so you can erase them.

1

2

A black outline makes it stand out.

White streaks make it shiny.

Curved lines make the arms and legs seem rounded.

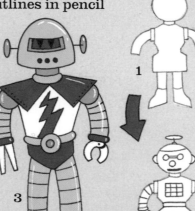

3

1

You could use markers instead of paint for a similar effect.

3

Draw a black patch for the robot's shadow.

2

Add shoe-laces.

3. Fill in the rest of the figure with shade 3. Add white paint to any parts you want to stand out.

Shade 3

Let the paint dry before adding shade 4.

4. Now take shade 4 and paint the areas that the light hits, blending the colors as before.

Shade 4

Vary the pressure on your pencil crayon.

Hatching

5. Add white crayon to the middle of the light areas. Don't overdo it, or you will lose the shiny effect.

Let some paint show through.

# Transformers®

Some robots can turn into other things such as cars. These are called Transformers®. Parts such as wheels are cleverly disguised on the robots' bodies so you would never guess they had other uses. Here, one robot is turning into a race car and another, into a rocket.

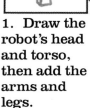

1. Draw the robot's head and torso, then add the arms and legs.

2. Add the parts shown here in red.

3. Draw in the face and add details to the body.

The robot has no neck.

Its lower arms pivot at the elbow.

Could these be wheels?

## Race car Transformer®

This Transformer® looks very tricky. If you copy the outlines one step at a time, though, you will end up with a very impressive series of pictures. Use a fairly hard pencil (see page 2).

## Rocket Transformer®

One way to copy shapes is to use a grid. Usually, you first need to draw a grid on tracing paper and lay it over the picture, but here it has been drawn for you.

1. Draw another grid with the same number of squares as the grid over the main picture. For a large picture, make the squares big.

2. Now look closely at the picture. Copy the shape inside each square until you have drawn the whole robot. Erase the squares.

The robot's wide chest will form the middle of the rocket.

The robot's pointed body disguises the rocket's nose.

Enormous feet hide the rocket's engines.

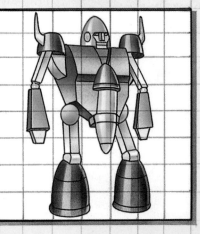

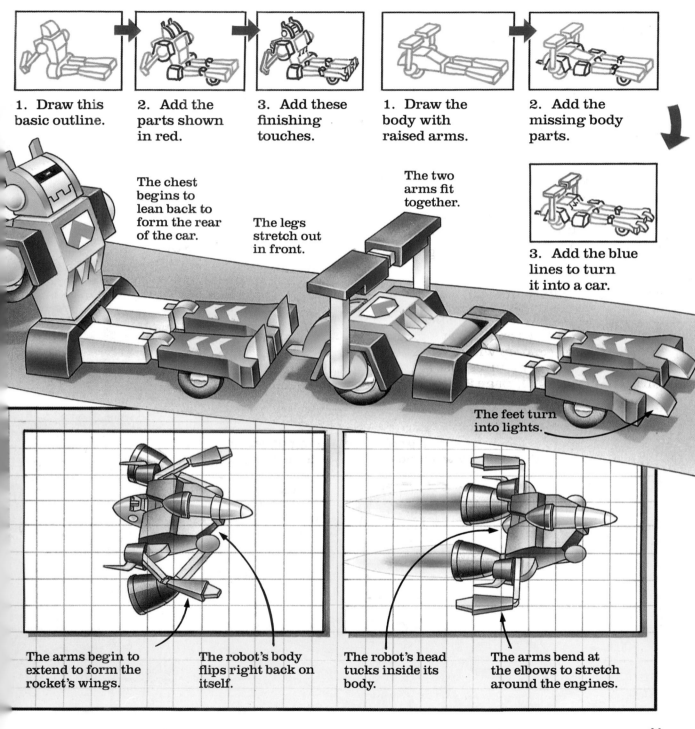

1. Draw this basic outline.

2. Add the parts shown in red.

3. Add these finishing touches.

1. Draw the body with raised arms.

2. Add the missing body parts.

3. Add the blue lines to turn it into a car.

The chest begins to lean back to form the rear of the car.

The legs stretch out in front.

The two arms fit together.

The feet turn into lights.

The arms begin to extend to form the rocket's wings.

The robot's body flips right back on itself.

The robot's head tucks inside its body.

The arms bend at the elbows to stretch around the engines.

# Useful robots

Imagine having no more chores. Instead, you would just program your robot to do them for you. . .

Below are a number of robots at work. You could also invent robots suited to your least favorite task.

## Housework helpers

These two robots are particularly well-suited to their work. Use the outlines below to help you draw them, then color them with pencil crayons.

Smart Bow tie.

Handsome figure to impress guests.

Big hands for balancing the tray.

Build up the darker areas with lots of strokes, all in the same direction. Erase the parts you want to be shiny.

Egg-shaped body to store the dirt.

Big nose to suck up dirt.

## Factory worker robots

Robots can be useful in factories. Robotic arms are used to help build cars, for example. They can do jobs that people find boring.

This scene shows robots creating other robots. First copy the conveyor belt, then use the outlines to help you draw the robotic arms.

Draw the green lines first.

1
2
3

See pages 8-9 for tips on how to paint the robots so they look shiny.

Add as many screws, bolts and springs as you like.

This foot is a little bigger than the other one because it is closer to you.

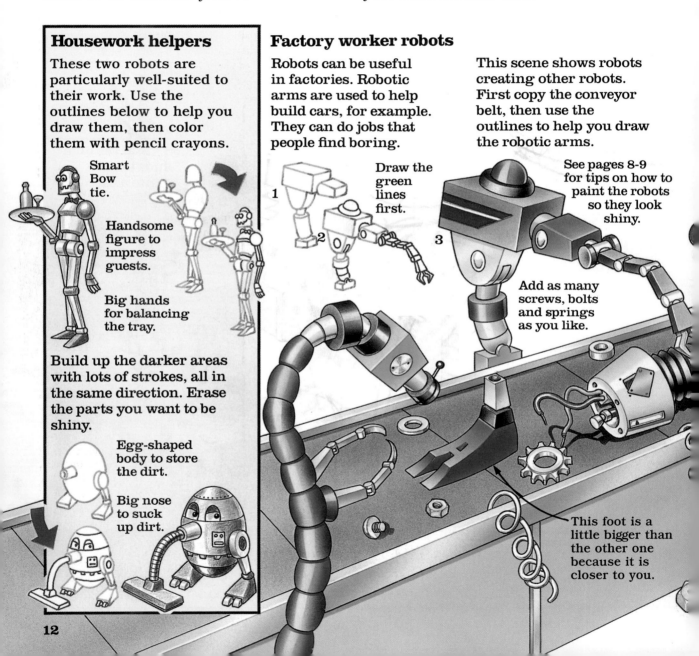

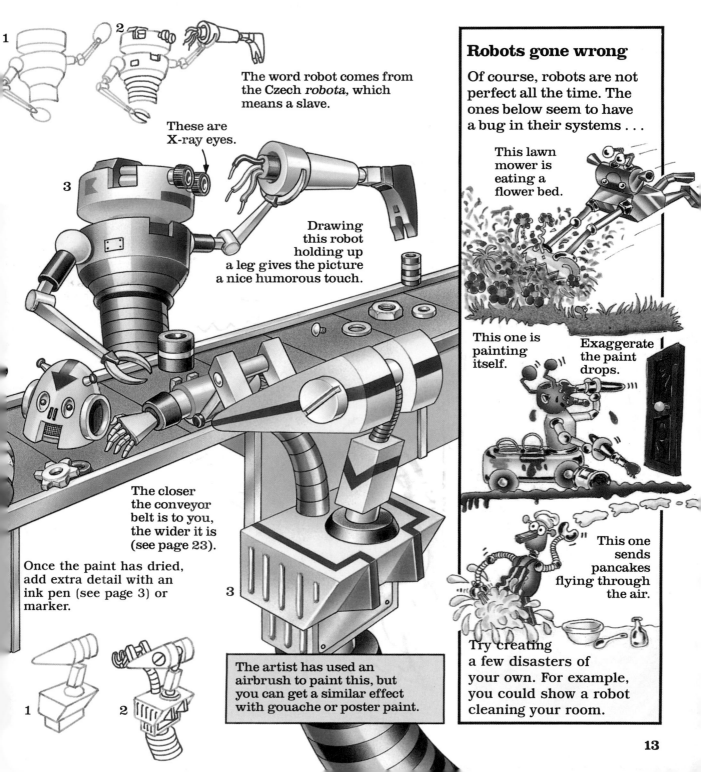

The word robot comes from the Czech *robota*, which means a slave.

These are X-ray eyes.

Drawing this robot holding up a leg gives the picture a nice humorous touch.

The closer the conveyor belt is to you, the wider it is (see page 23).

Once the paint has dried, add extra detail with an ink pen (see page 3) or marker.

The artist has used an airbrush to paint this, but you can get a similar effect with gouache or poster paint.

## Robots gone wrong

Of course, robots are not perfect all the time. The ones below seem to have a bug in their systems . . .

This lawn mower is eating a flower bed.

This one is painting itself.

Exaggerate the paint drops.

This one sends pancakes flying through the air.

Try creating a few disasters of your own. For example, you could show a robot cleaning your room.

13

# First aliens

The aliens on these two pages are quite simple. All you have to do is draw a few circular shapes, and you are halfway there . . .

## Goofy alien

1. Draw two large ovals, overlapping each other. Add circles for the joints and hands, then draw sticks for the limbs.

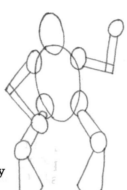

The legs gradually get wider.

You need two shades of each color, one light and one dark.

See the other ideas for eyes on the left.

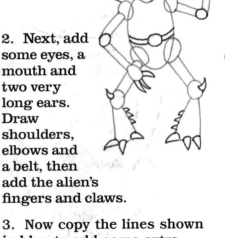

2. Next, add some eyes, a mouth and two very long ears. Draw shoulders, elbows and a belt, then add the alien's fingers and claws.

3. Now copy the lines shown in blue to add some extra details to the alien's clothes and body. Finally, color her in with crayons, following the tips on the right.

## Alien eyes

You can change your alien's mood by just adding a couple of lines to her eyes.

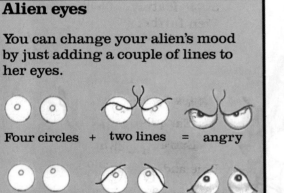

Four circles + two lines = angry

Four circles + two lines = sad

Four circles + two lines = tired

Four circles + two lines = worried

Four circles + four lines = surprised

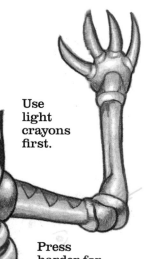

Use light crayons first.

Press harder for shadows.

Go over the shadows again with a darker color.

For highlights, leave some areas uncolored.

Go around the whole figure with black crayon.

## Mischievous alien

1. Draw an oval for the face, then place a triangular shape over its lower half. Add the neck and shoulders.

The lower half of the oval is not on the next picture, so erase it.

2. Now add the alien's eyes, nose, and mouth. Draw two lines beside the eyes and neck, then give him horns and spikes.

3. Finally, add the alien's teeth. You can then draw in his arms and chest if you like. Color him in with pencil crayons or markers.

## Alien friends

You can have a lot of fun turning your friends into aliens. Start by drawing a caricature.

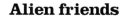

Carrot-top hair

Sticking-out ears

Long chin

A caricature, such as the picture above, exaggerates someone's main features.

Now draw an alien with these features, exaggerated even further and colored in an extraordinary alien way.

Antenna

Extended forehead

Enormous ears

Extra-long chin

Blue and orange coloring.

Here are a few other people with their alien counterparts.

# Friend or foe?

How do you make an alien look friendly? A smile is not enough: he may be contemplating his next meal – you. For example, look at the portraits of the four aliens on these pages. Two of them may be friendly, the others are not. Before reading the words, decide which ones are your enemies.

## Deceptive appearances

This cartoon alien seems too small to harm you. But wait . . .

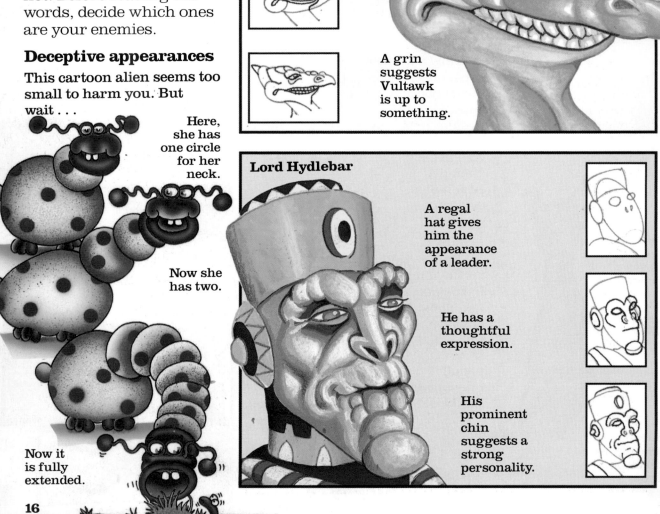

Here, she has one circle for her neck.

Now she has two.

Now it is fully extended.

**Vultawk**

Slit eyes look cunning and possibly evil.

The sharp face could be spiteful.

A grin suggests Vultawk is up to something.

**Lord Hydlebar**

A regal hat gives him the appearance of a leader.

He has a thoughtful expression.

His prominent chin suggests a strong personality.

## Solero

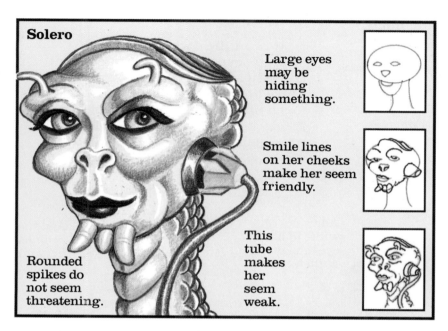

Large eyes may be hiding something.

Smile lines on her cheeks make her seem friendly.

This tube makes her seem weak.

Rounded spikes do not seem threatening.

## Drummader

Strong lines make him seem powerful.

Although he faces you, his eye will not meet yours.

His teeth are razor-sharp.

His mouth is enormous.

## Coloring the aliens

Choosing what you will color each alien with is very important. Here, you can see why.

Watercolors are good for making Vultawk's skin seem very smooth. This helps to give him a cold, slippery look.

Gouache makes Lord Hydlebar look slick. Leave a dark gap between his lips to show he has no teeth.

Pencil crayon gives Solero soft edges to make her look gentle. Lots of dark curves on her neck look like warts.

Use wax crayons for Drummader's leathery skin and rough armor. White highlights make his skin look sweaty.

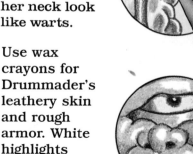

# Aliens on the move

How do aliens get around? Some might dart or leap, others might slither along in their slime. Some lucky aliens might even have space buggies.

These aliens were colored using an airbrush. You can also get good results with watercolors and crayons. For instance, follow the tips on the right to color the alien below.

## True slime

First paint the darker areas with a layer of deep greeny-blue watercolor. Let the paint dry, then go over the whole body with a lighter shade. Now touch up the shady areas again with the darker color. Add small dabs of white paint to look like light glistening on the alien's wet skin.

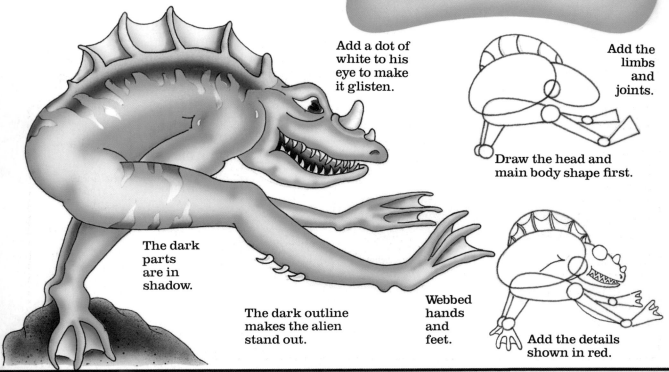

Add a dot of white to his eye to make it glisten.

Add the limbs and joints.

Draw the head and main body shape first.

The dark parts are in shadow.

The dark outline makes the alien stand out.

Webbed hands and feet.

Add the details shown in red.

## Fast-action wall frieze

For this frieze, use the outlines for the alien above but change the position of each body part as he moves.

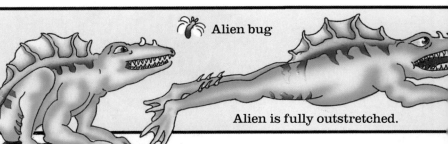

Alien bug

Alien is fully outstretched.

## Creepy-crawly alien

Draw this alien using the two outlines below to help you get the shape right. Go around the alien in brown pencil crayon, then color her in.

Circles for the joints.

Three tubes for each leg.

Your alien could be a different color.

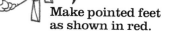

Make pointed feet as shown in red.

First paint a layer of pale watercolor over the body. Let it dry, then add shading in pencil crayon, in a deeper color. Draw dark hairs on top. Bald patches and tufts of hair look creepier than hair all over.

Make the hairs look ragged.

## Alien space buggy

Construct this space buggy one shape at a time, using the outlines on the far right. Add the alien last of all.

You can color the buggy with watercolor or poster paint. You could then put some mounds or craters in the background.

Start by drawing the boxes.

Add the circular shapes.

Erase the extra lines.

Thick grooves help the buggy travel across rough ground.

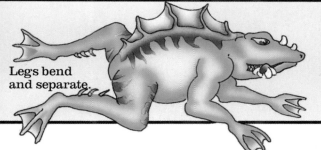

Legs bend and separate.

You could figure out further stages in between the positions shown here.

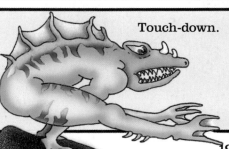

Touch-down.

19

# Aliens at play

What do you think aliens would do for fun? Play sports? Watch television? Go to the movies or a rock concert?

These pictures show some rather unusual rock musicians and an equally weird fan. The artist colored them using an airbrush. You could color yours by putting down several flat layers of watercolor or colored ink. When these are dry, add shading with pencil crayons. For a slightly paler look, just use pencil crayons.

White patches make this bald head look shiny.

Soft-edged highlights make the alien's body look rounded.

## Singer

1. As you can see, the singer's outline is mostly made up of rounded shapes.

A white highlight makes the eyes come alive.

Hard-edged, streaky highlights make the guitar look hard and flat.

2. Refine her outline as shown in red. Then add detail to her face, hands, toes and bodysuit.

## Guitarist

1. Sketch the alien's body shapes, then the guitar.

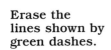

Erase the lines shown by green dashes.

2. Refine the outline and add more detail as shown in red.

## Aliens at work

These cartoon aliens are particularly suited to their type of work.

Hairdresser

Traffic policeman

Lifeguard

**Drummer**

## Alien boogie-woogie

This alien is obviously enjoying the music. His arms swinging one way while he is looking the other way help to make his pose look energetic. One foot off the floor also gives a sense of movement.

The head, knee and right foot are in a straight line.

A sharp angle here looks dramatic.

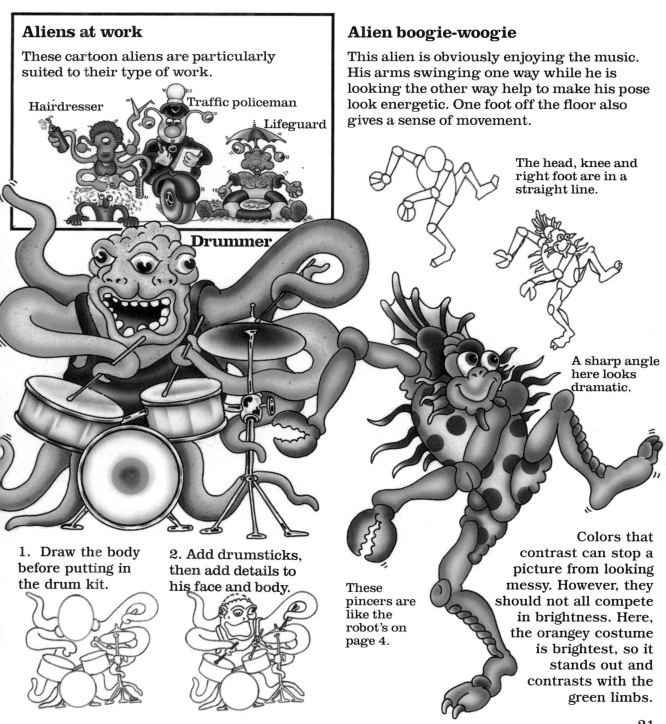

1. Draw the body before putting in the drum kit.

2. Add drumsticks, then add details to his face and body.

These pincers are like the robot's on page 4.

Colors that contrast can stop a picture from looking messy. However, they should not all compete in brightness. Here, the orangey costume is brightest, so it stands out and contrasts with the green limbs.

# Spaceships

What do spaceships look like? It may depend on what they are designed for. For instance, a police spaceship would need to be fast, whereas it would be more important for a family spaceship to be comfortable.

The spaceships on these two pages are airbrushed, which gives them a very smooth finish. You could use poster paints for a bold effect.

## Police spaceship

This spaceship is designed for the alien police force. Its saucer shape enables it to do quick U-turns, and the revolving chair and circular glass dome give the pilot all-around vision. It has three powerful engines for speedy chases.

White highlights follow the spaceship's curves. Their hard edges make the surface look smooth.

Pale blue edges look like reflections in the glass dome.

## Taking off and landing

These cartoon spaceships are about to launch or to land. How do you think the three large spaceships on these pages might take off or land? You could draw them in action.

This flying saucer is thrust upwards by lots of thin jets of water.

The spaceship below lands by dropping down massive feet.

This is propelled by a launching pad that works like a trampoline.

Paint white highlights along this edge.

To blend tones, add the second color while the first is still damp.

Draw the main body, then the engines.

Add an alien and details to the ship.

## Touro-spaceship

This spaceship is designed for cruising around. It has plenty of windows for sightseeing, and has four long legs for soft landings. It is slow, but economical on fuel and also very comfortable.

A yellow light makes it look warm inside.

Start with the dome.

Add the windows, door and legs as shown in red.

You could add shading with crayon instead of paint.

## About perspective

Have you noticed how things look smaller as they get further away? This is called perspective. For example, the time travel ship's wings look shorter at the back than at the front.

Vanishing point.

If you continued the lines representing the tips of the wings, they would eventually meet. This is known as the vanishing point.

## Time travel spaceship

This spaceship whizzes through space with the minimum of air resistance. The dark glass windshield makes it look mysterious, because you cannot see the pilot.

Turbo engines

The main shape.

Add the red lines.

The stronger colors on this spaceship make it look more aggressive.

Make the wings really thin for a streamlined look.

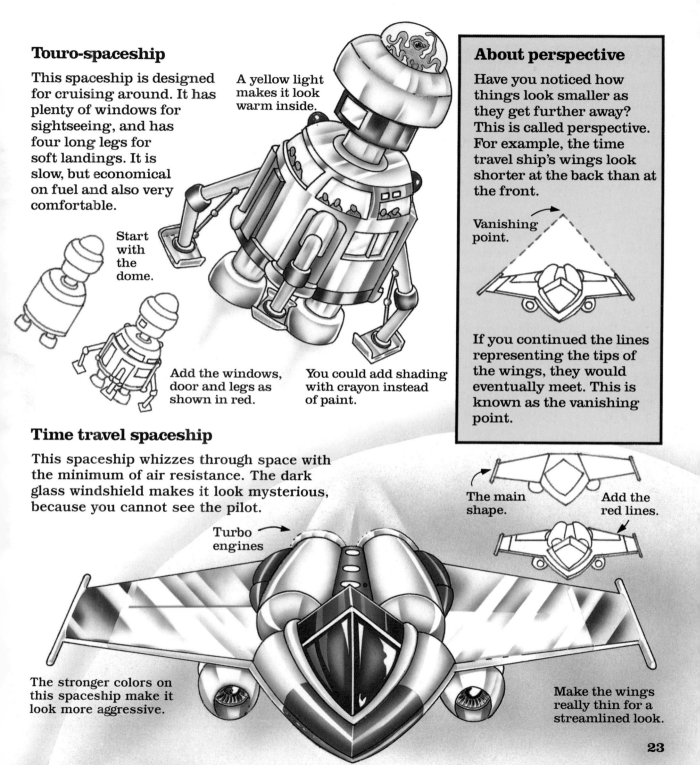

# Aliens on Earth

How would you react if you saw an alien spaceship landing on the street? What would an alien think of you and your planet? Here are a few ideas . . .

## Drawing the spaceship

1. Start by drawing an upside-down hat, then add some curved lines. Draw the aliens, starting with their heads, then their chests and arms.

2. Show the aliens' faces inside the helmets. Draw in their spacesuits, then add fins and stabilizers to the ship. Now give the aliens some fingers.

3. Add lights and more stabilizers, then draw tubes coming out of the helmets. Finally, add the finishing touches to the aliens shown in blue.

Use paint to make the sky really flat.

Use wax crayon for the larger areas.

The aliens' faces are colored with pencil crayon.

Keep the background uncluttered so the ship stands out.

Use purple for the shady parts of the ship, red next to this, then pink where light hits.

## Comic strips

A comic strip is a fun way to tell a story. This strip is about a group of aliens landing on Earth. Around it are tips to help you create your own strip. Strong, fairly flat colors look good in comic strips.

Sounds help it come to life.

A short caption sets the scene.

The different frame shapes add interest.

A FLYING SAUCER BLASTS THROUGH SPACE TOWARDS . . . EARTH!

EARTH

VAROOM

TOUCHDOWN!

Shade the fronts of the buildings in yellow, the sides in orangey-brown.

Add windows using pencil crayon.

You could show the aliens landing on your house.

Leave the highlighted parts uncolored.

Go around the outlines with a dark color.

## Alien reactions

By altering a few lines on an alien's face, you can make her worried, amused or scared stiff.

A furrowed forehead shows she is frowning.

Wrinkles on the sides of her forehead emphasize her raised eyebrows.

Her mouth is almost straight.

**Worried alien**

The mouth curls upwards in a smile.

**Amused alien**

Eyes are wide open.

Open eyebrows are raised really high.

Her mouth is open in a gasp.

**Terrified alien**

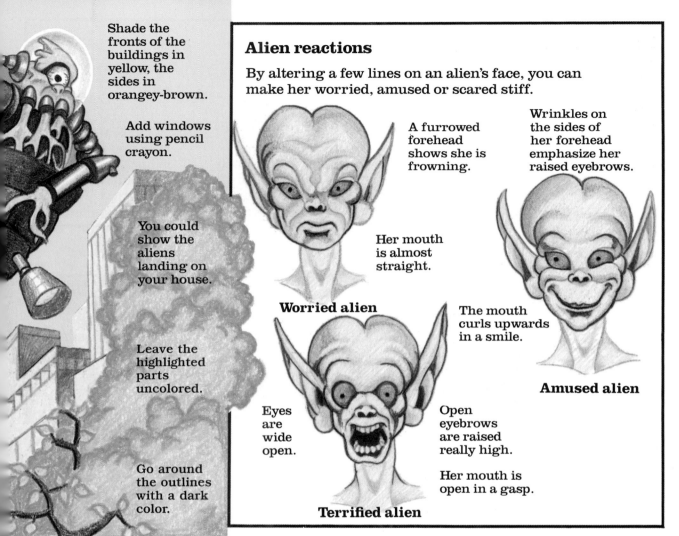

This reinforces their bewilderment.

This sweat adds humor.

A jagged edge suggests he is really alarmed.

Pictures tell the story, not words.

WHAT A STRANGE, BARREN PLANET!

SUDDENLY...

YIKES! QUICK, BACK TO THE SHIP!

SCRATCH! SCRATCH!

# An alien town

You can have fun dreaming up ideas for a town in outer space. This scene will start you off. You might also like to add things from elsewhere in the book.

Instead of copying the outlines, you could use the grid method described on page 10. You will first need to draw a grid on tracing paper and tape it to the picture.

## Monorail

1. Draw three lines for the track, then add the cars and pylons. Draw a tunnel entrance.

2. Decorate the cars and the tunnel, then continue the monorail track in the distance.

## Barber's shop

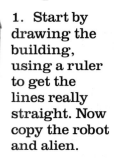

1. Start by drawing the building, using a ruler to get the lines really straight. Now copy the robot and alien.

2. Give the alien a shaggy coat, dress the robot and fill in his face. Now add the details to the chair, pipes and building.

Paint blue and gray streaks across the barber's window.

Vanishing point (see page 23).

Things become less distinct the further away they are.

Space helmets filter out poisonous gases.

The ground is so smooth and clean that it looks unreal.

## Alien plants

1. Draw a tall tin can with a circle in one corner. Add spiral rings around it.

2. Erase the can, then add branches, fruit and thorns to the tree.

Here are some alien flowers. You could add them to your picture.

## A robot's house

1. Draw a hut shape for the ground floor, then add the second floor. Now draw in the satellite dish.

2. Next, draw some circles between the floors, then add a door. Position an antenna on the satellite dish, then add some curved lines on the roof.

3. Draw the windows and curtains. You could add a robot waving from one of the windows. Finally, add some pipes to connect the circles.

To make this plant look really sci-fi, add highlights so it shines.

Paint masses of dark thorns on the fruit. Add white streaks to them.

For a tongue-in-cheek effect, show robots and aliens doing things humans might do in real life.

This curved door looks weird.

You could replace this spaceship with one from pages 22-23.

# Robots on the movie screen

Have you ever wondered how the robots that you see in movies and on television are created? These two pages show their journey from just names in a script to the amazing creatures you see on-screen.

## Drawing the robot

First, the director gives the script to a team that specializes in creating robots. They talk over their ideas for how the robot should look with an artist. The artist then starts work on the drawings.

The team discusses what they like or dislike about the drawings. For example, should it be cuter? Taller? More aggressive? The artist produces something everyone is happy with.

Here are three drawings by Syd Mead for the robot "Number Five" in the movie *Short Circuit*.*

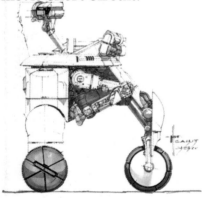

The designs above and below are less appealing than the robot shown on the right.

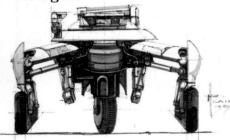

The final drawing. Small changes were later made as the robot was being built.

A laser on one side gives the robot a lop-sided appeal.

A spindly body shows the audience that no actor is hiding inside.

This lies flat when Number Five needs to crouch down and hide.

Batteries hide in here.

A tread system gives Number Five a military look (in the movie, he was originally built to fight wars).

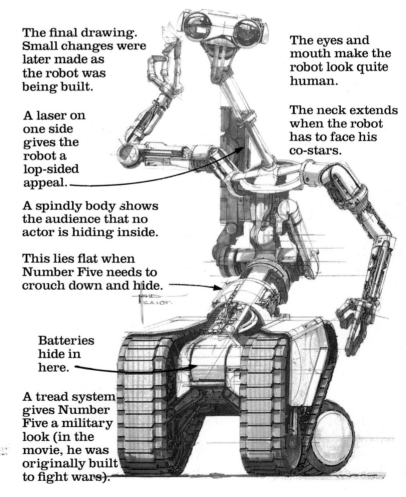

The eyes and mouth make the robot look quite human.

The neck extends when the robot has to face his co-stars.

*The film *Short Circuit* and the character Number Five ©1986 TriStar Pictures Inc.

## Making a 3-D model

The team creates a model like the one on the right. They discuss the tasks it will perform. Electrical and mechanical engineers draw blueprints (designs) to show how gears and so on work.

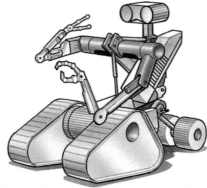

3-D model of Number Five.

The model is made out of basic materials such as paper, plastic and wood.

## Building the robot

Working from the blueprints, technicians now build some of the more complicated parts of the robot. They show the film director how the eyes will move, the head tilt and so on.

If you pull ▶ on these three cables . . .

. . . Number ▶ Five's fingers will start to move.

Finally, they build a number of identical finished robots so that filming will not be held up if one breaks down. For *Short Circuit*, there were 15 identical models of Number Five.

This is Number Five with the man in charge of designing him, Eric Allard. Eric is wearing a radio-controlled device known as an upper-body telemetry suit. When he moves his arms or chest, Number Five moves in the same way.

### On the set

Although some of the maneuvers you see on-screen are performed by a radio-controlled robot, many of the close-up ones are done by puppeteers working a robot puppet.

Actress Ally Sheedy rehearsing a scene with a Number Five puppet. The television screens give the puppeteers live footage of the robot's movements.

A radio-controlled Number Five practicing going up and down steps.

# Mix and match

Here is an assortment of heads, chests and legs for you to mix and match. Also, here you can find some further ideas for space vehicle outlines.

The shapes at the top and bottom of the opposite page might inspire you when constructing robots and aliens from your own imagination. The robot pieces can help when drawing things from odd angles, too.

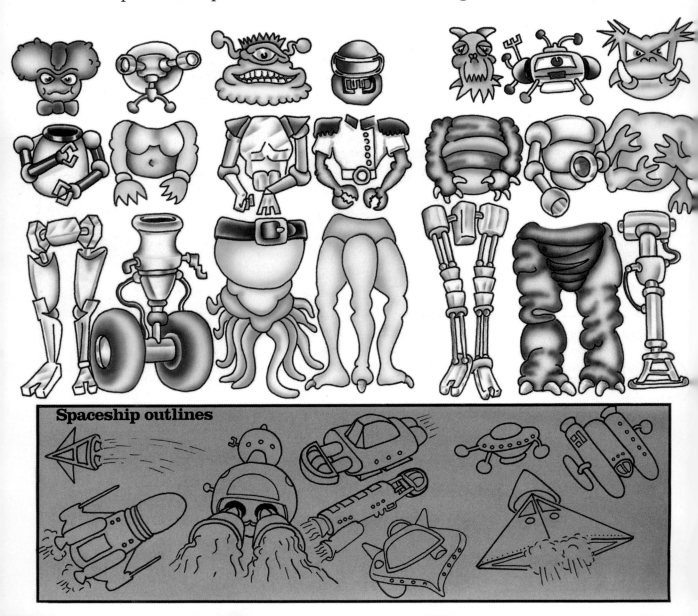

**Spaceship outlines**

# Alien shapes

## Space buggy outlines

## Robot pieces

# Index